Writing Skills

Grade 2

FlashKids
New York

Harcourt Family Learning™

FLASH KIDS and the distinctive Flash Kids logo are registered trademarks of Barnes and Noble Booksellers, Inc.
Harcourt Family Learning and Design is a trademark of Harcourt, Inc.

© 2006 Flash Kids
Adapted from *Experiences with Writing Styles Grade 2*
© 1998 Steck-Vaughn Company
Licensed under special arrangement with Harcourt Achieve.

For more information, please visit flashkids.com
Please submit all inquiries to Flashkids@sterlingpublishing.com

ISBN 978-1-4114-0480-9

Manufactured in China

Lot #:
32 34 36 38 40 39 37 35 33 31
07/18

Illustrated by Clive Scruton

Dear Parent,

Reading and writing well are essential tools for success in all school subjects. In addition, many states now include writing assessments in their standardized tests. There may be no precise formula for good writing, but through studying samples and practicing different styles, your child will build the skills and versatility to approach any writing assignment with ease and confidence.

Each of the six units in this fun, colorful workbook focuses on a unique type of writing that your second-grader may be required to use in school or may wish to pursue in his or her free time. These types include sentence about a picture, personal story, friendly letter, paragraph that describes, story, and how-to paragraph. The first half of each unit reinforces writing aspects such as putting pictures into sentences, using descriptive words, identifying problems and solutions, and using proofreading marks, in addition to providing fun, inspirational writing ideas for your child to explore alone or with a friend. The second half of most units focuses on a practice paper or paragraph that exemplifies the writing type. After your child reads the practice passage, he or she will analyze it, prepare a writing plan for his or her own paper or paragraph, write a first draft, revise it, and, lastly, allow you or a friend to score it.

Here are some helpful suggestions for getting the most out of this workbook:

- Provide a quiet place to work.
- Go over the directions together.
- Encourage your child to do his or her best.
- Check each activity when it is complete.
- Review your child's work together, noting good work as well as points for improvement.

As your child completes the units, help him or her maintain a positive attitude about writing. Provide writing opportunities such as a journal, in which your child can write about things that happen each day and can keep a running list of topics or story ideas for future writing projects. Read your child's stories aloud at bedtime, and display his or her writing in your home.

Most importantly, enjoy this time you spend together. Your child's writing skills will improve even more with your dedication and support!

Proofreading Marks

Use the following symbols to help make proofreading faster.

MARK	MEANING	EXAMPLE
◯	spell correctly	Today is a (specail) day. *special*
⊙	add period	It is Kevin's birthday⊙
?	add question mark	What kind of pet do you have?
≡	capitalize	My dog's name is scooter.
℘	take out	He likes to ~~to~~ run and play.
∧	add	He even likes to get ∧ bath. *a*
¶	indent paragraph	¶ I love my dog, Scooter. He is the best pet I have ever had. Every morning he wakes me with a bark. Every night he sleeps with me.
⌄ ⌄	add quotation marks	⌄You are my best friend,⌄ I tell him.

Table of Contents

UNIT 1: Sentence about a Picture

HOW MUCH DO YOU KNOW?

Look at each picture. Draw a circle around the group of words that is a complete sentence.

1. The girl eats pizza.

   A slice of pizza

2. a robot and a dog

   The robot walks a dog.

Finish the sentence with the more exact word.

3. Mai eats _____ for breakfast.
   (cereal, food)

Studying a Sentence about a Picture

- A sentence tells a complete thought.
- It begins with a capital letter.
- It ends with a special mark.

Look at each picture. Draw a circle around the group of words that is a complete sentence.

1. The balloon goes up.

   man in it

2. a messy room

   The room is a mess!

3. It's a windy fall day.

   an open store

4. a good lunch

   The girls are ready to eat.

Using Details to Tell the Main Idea

- To write a sentence about a picture, good writers look at all the details first.
- Then they put the details together to tell the main idea.

Look at the pictures. Draw a line under the details you see in the pictures. Then draw a line under the sentence that tells the main idea.

1.

DETAILS

fruit bowl	2 eggs
bird cage	1 glass
bedroom	2 sinks

MAIN IDEA

One person will eat breakfast.
Fruit tastes really good!

2.

DETAILS

ticket booth	Ferris wheel
monkeys	children
roller coaster	cotton candy

MAIN IDEA
The fair is open!
I lost my ticket!

Using Exact Words

Good writers use exact words to give a reader more information.

Finish each sentence with the more exact word.

1. _____ sit in the trees.
   (Animals, Chimpanzees)

2. They are _____ for food.
   (looking, hunting)

3. _____ are the best.
   (Bananas, Fruits)

4. Can they see those big _____ bunches?
   (bright, yellow)

5. Watch the chimpanzees _____ !
   (leap, move)

Proofreading Sentences

PROOFREADING HINTS

- Be sure your sentence begins with a capital letter.
- Be sure your sentence ends with an end mark.

Read each sentence. Use the Proofreading Marks to correct the five mistakes. Write the sentences correctly.

PROOFREADING MARKS

⬭	spell correctly
⊙	add period
?	add question mark
≡	capitalize
℘	take out
∧	add
¶	indent paragraph
⌄ ⌄	add quotation marks

See the chart on page 4 to learn how to use these marks.

1. bears are big animals.

2. They may weigh 1,000 pounds

3. some live in cold places

4. others like warm weather.

1. _____

2. _____

3. _____

4. _____

My Favorite Food

Draw a picture of your favorite food. Think of a sentence about it. Write the sentence. Show your picture to a friend. Read your sentence aloud. Tell what makes it a complete sentence.

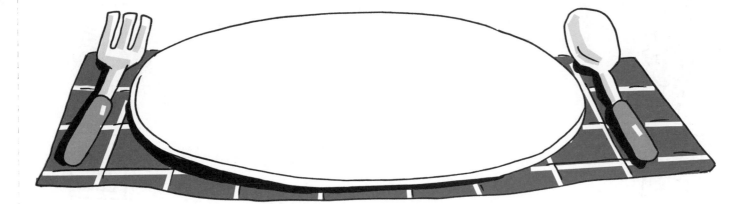

_____

_____

_____

First Place

Imagine that you just won first place in your favorite sport. What prize did you win? Draw a picture of your prize. Write a sentence to tell about your picture.

_____

_____

_____

Going on an Outing

Think of someplace you would like to go with your class. Draw a picture of the place. Then write a sentence about it.

_____

_____

_____

A Favorite Day

The picture shows Ann's favorite day. Look at the picture. Write a sentence about Ann's favorite day.

_____

_____

_____

Finish the Picture

Finish the picture. Draw what happens. Then write a sentence about the picture.

_____

_____

_____

Write about a Circus

Imagine that you are in a circus. What would you do?
Draw a picture of yourself. Write a sentence to go with
the picture.

_____

_____

_____

On a Trip

Pretend that you are on a trip. Draw a picture of something you see. Write a sentence about it.

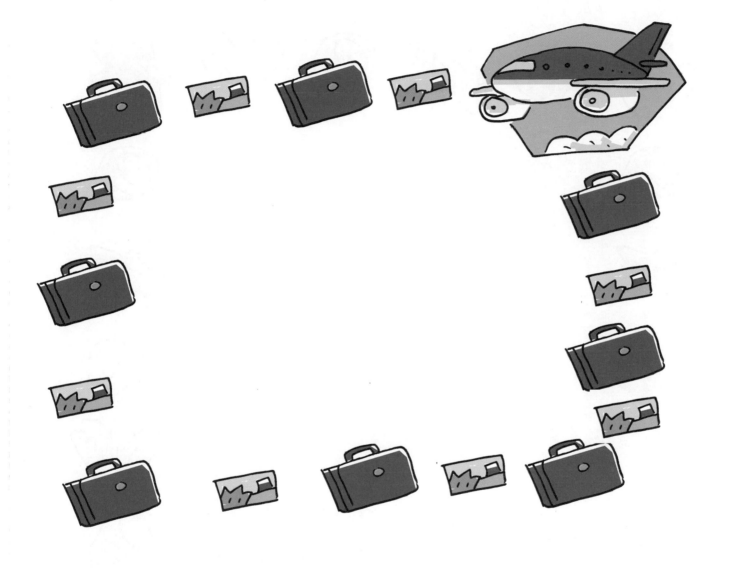

_____

_____

_____

At the Beach

Imagine you are at the beach. Draw a picture of something you might do there. Then write a sentence about it.

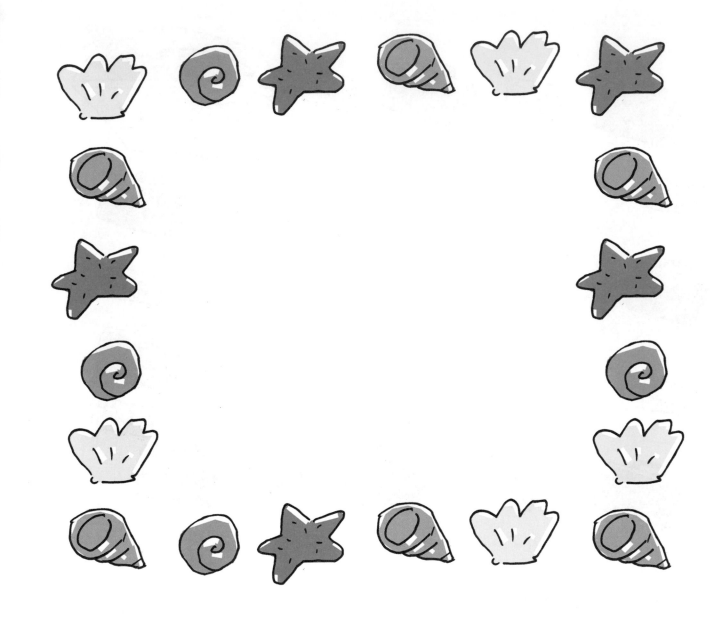

_____

_____

_____

On a Nature Hike

Pretend that you are on a hike through a forest. Draw a picture of something you might see on your hike. Write a sentence about it.

_____

_____

_____

Someone Special

Think about someone who is special to you. Draw a picture
of that person. Then write a sentence about him or her.

_____

_____

_____

My Favorite Animal

Think about your favorite animal. Draw a picture of that animal. Write a sentence telling what you like about that animal.

_____

_____

_____

I Can Do That

Everyone has special talents, or things they can do well. Some talents might be playing an instrument, playing sports, or solving puzzles. Draw a picture of one of your special talents. Then write a sentence about it.

_____

_____

_____

Tell about It

Look at the picture. Write a sentence that explains what happened.

_____

_____

_____

UNIT 2: Personal Story

HOW MUCH DO YOU KNOW?

Read the story. Circle the words that tell the order in which things happen.

My family had fun at the summer fair yesterday. First, my brother rode a scary ride. Then, my sister and I got to pet a goat! The goat tried to bite my shirt. The goat made us laugh! Last of all, I won a prize at the fair. I can't wait for the next fair!

Write the sentence that tells what the topic is.

TOPIC SENTENCE

_____

_____

Studying a Personal Story

- A personal story tells about something you have done.
- It can tell how you feel about something.
- A story tells what happened in order.
- It uses the words <u>I</u>, <u>me</u>, <u>my</u>, <u>we</u>, and <u>our</u>.

Read the story. Draw a line under the words that show it is a personal story. Draw a circle around the words that tell the order in which things happen.

My family and I love holidays. We think Thanksgiving is the best. All my grandparents come to our house. First, we sit at a very long table. Then, my sister brings in the food. The turkey always smells great! It tastes even better. After dinner, we sing songs. We have a good time. Last of all, we hug each other good-bye. I can't wait for the next holiday!

Write a sentence about your favorite holiday.

_____

_____

_____

Grouping Ideas by Topic

- In a personal story, good writers tell about one topic.
- Good writers use only details that tell about the topic.

Read the story about animal movies. Write the sentence that tells what the topic is. Draw a line under the details that tell about the topic.

    I like many movies about animals. In one movie I saw deer, bears, and foxes in a forest. Another movie was a cartoon about mice and pigs. The best animal movie I ever saw took place in the jungle. It was about a parrot that saved a tiger's life. It was really great!

TOPIC SENTENCE

_____

_____

Write a sentence to add to the story.

_____

_____

_____

Using Synonyms

> Good writers choose words to write exactly
> what they mean to say.

Read each sentence. Choose the more exact word to finish the sentence.

1. We _____ into the store before it rains.
   (go, dash)

2. There are many _____ on the shelves.
   (boxes, things)

3. My dad buys some ripe _____ .
   (fruit, apples)

4. I find some _____ peaches.
   (soft, fuzzy)

5. I feel _____ when I'm with my dad.
   (cheerful, good)

6. My dad makes me _____ .
   (laugh, giggle)

Proofreading a Personal Story

PROOFREADING HINTS
- Be sure that the word <u>I</u> is a capital letter.
- Be sure that each sentence begins with a capital letter.
- Be sure that each sentence ends with an end mark.

Read the story. Use the Proofreading Marks to correct at least eight mistakes.

PROOFREADING MARKS

⬯	spell correctly
⊙	add period
?	add question mark
≡	capitalize
℘	take out
∧	add
¶	indent paragraph
⋁ ⋁	add quotation marks

One day my family and I went to an apple orchard. we went to pick fresh apples. first, i got a big basket. next, I picked some ripe apples off the trees I put them in the basket After about an hour, i was too hungry to keep going. that's when i bit into a juicy, red apple The sweet, ripe apple tasted better than anything else in the world.

Write about a Pet

Do you have a pet? If not, imagine that you have one. Where does your pet sleep? What does your pet play with? Write a story about your pet.

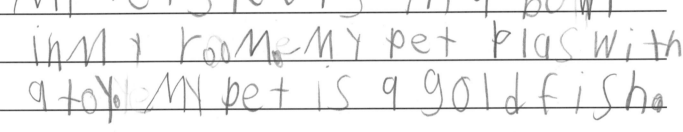

My pet sleeps in a bowl inn t room. My pet plas with a toy. My pet is a goldfish.

Fun with Your Neighbors

Think of something you like to do with your neighbors. Draw a picture of you doing it. Then write a story to go with your picture. Use the words <u>men</u>, <u>women</u>, and <u>children</u> in your sentences.

_____

_____

_____

_____

_____

_____

_____

I'm Late!

Think of a time when you were late. Write a story about what happened.

_____

_____

_____

_____

_____

_____

_____

_____

Write about Your Feelings

Choose a feeling you sometimes have. Draw a picture of yourself with that feeling. Below the picture, write a story about a time you felt that way.

_____

_____

_____

_____

_____

Write about a Sport

Think about a game you and a friend like to play. Write a story about a time you played the game.

_____

_____

_____

_____

Let's Eat!

Think of one of your favorite foods. Close your eyes and picture it in your mind. Then write words in the chart to describe the food.

FOOD: _____

_____   _____

_____   _____

_____   _____

_____   _____

Write a story about your favorite food.

_____

_____

_____

_____

_____

My Favorite Holiday

Think of four things that happen on your favorite holiday. Draw four pictures to show these things. Then write a story that tells what happens. Use your pictures to help you.

FIRST	NEXT

THEN	LAST

_____

_____

_____

_____

_____

A Practice Personal Story

SPELLING BEE

Last week I competed in the school spelling bee.

The contestants sat in three rows on the stage. At first, I

was not very nervous. Then, I looked up and saw that

the whole school had come to watch us take turns

spelling words aloud. Suddenly, my palms felt sweaty.

Soon, the spelling bee began. One at a time, each of us

stood at the microphone in the center of the stage. The

judge pronounced a word slowly. You had to spell it

correctly to stay in the contest. The judge began with a

list of easy words, but soon the words got harder. I had

to spell the word <u>acrobat</u>. I tried to picture it in my

mind. Then I started to spell aloud, but I said the letter <u>k</u>

instead of <u>c</u>. As soon as I said the wrong letter, I knew I had

made a mistake. But it was too late! Everyone clapped to

show they were proud of how hard I tried. I still smiled as I

left the stage. Of course, I was a little disappointed that I

did not win, but I will try again next year!

Respond to the Practice Story

After you read the story called "Spelling Bee," write your answers to the following questions.

1. What did the writer do last week?

_____

2. How did the writer show that he became nervous?

_____

3. How did the writer spell the word <u>acrobat</u> during the spelling bee?

_____

4. Did the writer win the spelling bee? How do you know?

_____

5. How did the writer feel at the end of the story?

_____

6. Using one or two sentences, summarize this story. Use these questions to help you:

   • What was the story about?
   • How does the story end?

_____

_____

_____

Writing Assignment

Think about three things you do before you leave the house each morning. Draw three pictures that show what you do first, next, and last. Then write a sentence that tells about each picture. Use this writing plan to help you write a first draft on the next page.

First Draft

TIPS FOR WRITING A PERSONAL NARRATIVE:

- Write from your point of view. Use the words <u>I</u>, <u>me</u> and <u>my</u> to show your readers that this is your story.

- Think about what you want to tell your reader.

- Organize your ideas into a beginning, middle, and end.

- Write an introduction that "grabs" your reader's attention.

- Write an ending for your story. Write it from your point of view.

Use your writing plan as a guide for writing a personal story. Include a catchy title.

_____

_____

_____

_____

_____

_____

(Continue on your own paper.)

Revise the Draft

Use the chart below to help you revise your draft. Check YES or NO to answer each question in the chart. If you answer NO, make notes to remind yourself how you can revise, or change, your writing to improve it.

Question	YES ✔	NO ✔	If the answer is NO, what will you do to improve your writing?
Does your story describe your morning routine?			
Does your story have a beginning?			
Do you describe events in the order they happened?			
Does your story have an ending?			
Did you add details to your story to make it interesting?			
Do you tell your story from your point of view?			
Have you corrected mistakes in spelling, grammar, and punctuation?			

Use the notes in your chart and your writing plan to revise your draft.

Writing Report Card

Read your revised draft again or ask someone else to read it. Have the person who reads your paper complete the following Report Card. Revise your paper until you have no less than a Very Good Score for each item.

Title of paper: _____

Purpose of paper: _This is a personal story. It tells about my morning routine._

Person who scores the paper: _____

Score	Writing Goals
	Does this story have a beginning?
	Are the events described in the order they happened?
	Is there an ending?
	Are there details to make the story interesting?
	Is the story told from the writer's point of view?
	Are the story's grammar, spelling, and punctuation correct?

☺ Excellent Score   ☆ Very Good Score   + Good Score
✔ Acceptable Score   − Needs Improvement

UNIT 3: Friendly Letter

HOW MUCH DO YOU KNOW?

Read the letter. Underline these parts of the letter.
Use different colors.

1. Use green to underline the heading.
2. Use blue to underline the signature.
3. Use red to underline the closing.

Then answer the question about the letter.

October 22, 2005

Dear Aunt Rosa,

    The sweater you knitted for my birthday is great! The fall days here have been chilly. It's nice to have a new warm sweater to wear. It is just the right size. Thank you, Aunt Rosa.

Love, Juan

4. Who wrote the letter?

_____

Studying a Friendly Letter

A friendly letter has five parts.

Read the letter. Draw a circle around each part of the letter.
Use different colors.

1. Circle the heading with red.
2. Circle the closing with yellow.
3. Circle the greeting with blue.
4. Circle the signature with orange.
5. Circle the body with green.

July 27, 2005

Dear Chris,

    My family and I moved to a new house. I go to another school now. My new teacher is nice. I have a friend named Jimmy. He is in my class. Jimmy and I are on the same baseball team. Do you like to play baseball?

Your friend,
Richard

Picturing Events

Good writers picture events in their minds
before they write about them.

Finish the pictures. Draw what happens. Then write what happens.

1.

_____

_____

_____

2.

_____

_____

_____

Writing for Your Reader

- Good writers decide <u>who</u> will read their writing.
- Good writers decide <u>why</u> they are writing.

Read the letter. Then answer the questions about it.

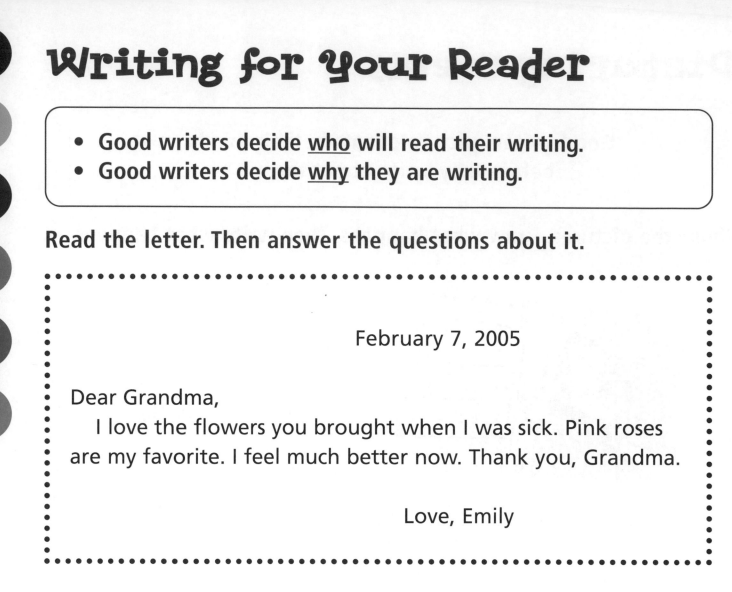

February 7, 2005

Dear Grandma,
    I love the flowers you brought when I was sick. Pink roses are my favorite. I feel much better now. Thank you, Grandma.

Love, Emily

1. To whom did Emily write the letter?

_____

2. Why did Emily write the letter?

_____

3. What did Emily write that Grandma might like to read?

_____

Joining Sentences

Writers often join two sentences into one.
The new sentence says the same thing in fewer words.

Read each pair of sentences. Use the
word **and** to join the two sentences
into one. The first one is done for you.

1. Andy talks. Andy tells jokes.

Andy talks and tells jokes.

2. He dances. He sings.

3. Andy writes plays. Andy acts them out.

4. He gets applause. He gets cheers.

Proofreading a Friendly Letter

PROOFREADING HINTS

- Check for commas in the heading, greeting, and closing.
- Check for capital letters in the heading, greeting, and closing.
- Check your spelling.

Read the letter. Add <u>commas</u> (,) where they are needed. Correct at least six mistakes. Use the Proofreading Marks.

PROOFREADING MARKS

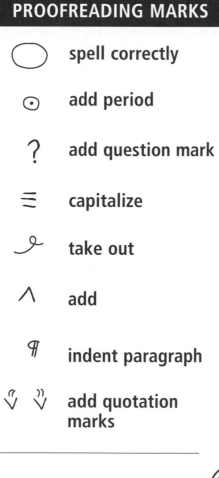

⬭	spell correctly
⊙	add period
?	add question mark
≡	capitalize
℘	take out
∧	add
¶	indent paragraph
˅ ˅	add quotation marks

February 7, 2005

dear Tanya

I had fun at your house last week! I'm so bezy at school now. I'm in the class play. I am a bear in the play My costume is brown and fuzzy. have you ever been in a play?

your friend
Brenda

Write about Summer Fun

Write a letter to a friend. Tell your friend what you like to do in the summer.

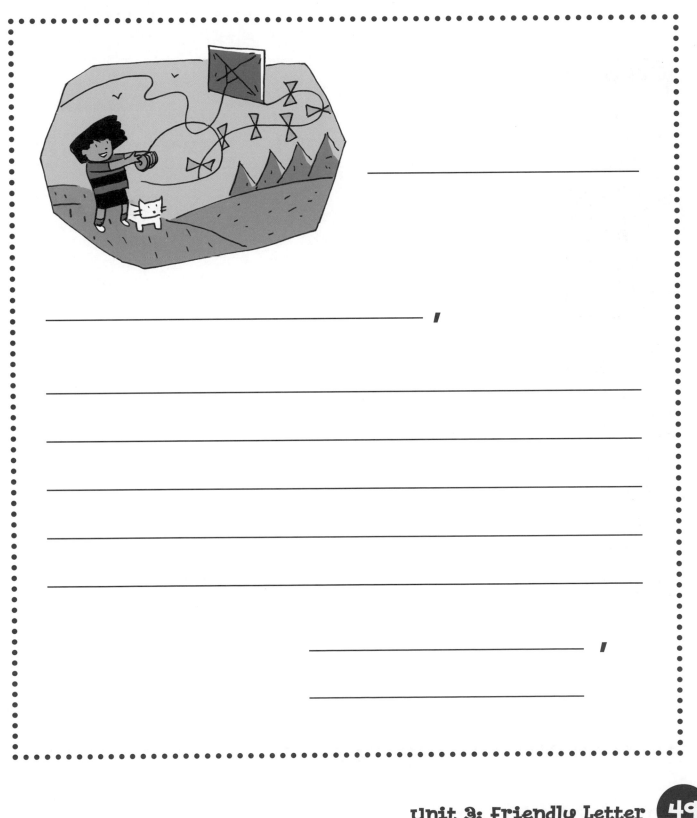

Write about a Visit

Think about a time you visited a friend or a relative. Write a letter to that friend or relative telling what you enjoyed about the visit.

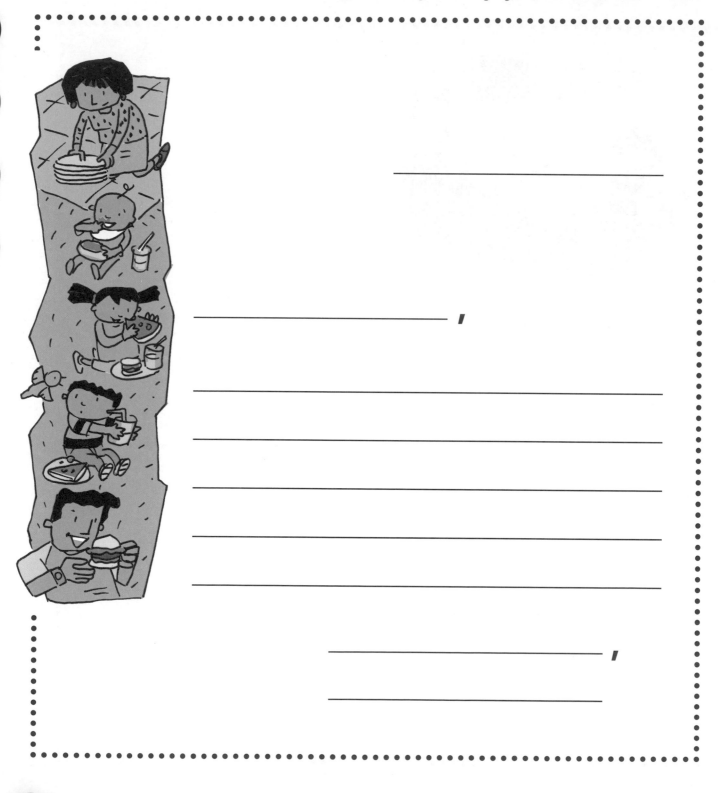

_____

_____ ,

_____

_____

_____

_____

_____ ,

_____

A Season Letter

Choose your favorite season. It might be fall, winter, spring, or summer. Draw a picture of your favorite season. Then write a letter to a friend telling something you would like to do during your favorite season.

My Favorite Season

_____

_____ ,

_____

_____

_____

_____

_____ ,

_____

A Letter to a Famous Person

Write a letter to a famous person. Tell that person something about yourself. Ask the person questions about what he or she does.

Invite a Friend

Write a letter to invite someone to do something or to go somewhere. Use these ideas or use your own ideas.

A CLASS PLAY   TO COME TO YOUR HOUSE

Thank You Very Much

With a friend, make a list of people at school who have helped you. Then pick someone from the list and write him or her a thank-you note.

-------------------------------   -------------------------------

-------------------------------   -------------------------------

-------------------------------   -------------------------------

THANK YOU!

-- ,

------------------------------------ ,

Good News!

Think about something you did well during your school day.
Write a letter to a family member to share the good news.

_____

_____

_____ ,

_____

_____

_____

_____

_____ ,

_____

A Practice Letter

Dear Kathryn,

We finally moved into our new house! It is a large farmhouse in the country. Our closest neighbors are two miles down the road. That is very different from our old neighborhood, but I am slowly getting used to it. Yesterday, my mom and I went on a walk down by the creek and we met a really nice girl named Shannon. She likes to go bike riding, just like you! I hope Shannon and I will be friends, but she could never replace you. I miss you so much. I hope you get to come visit soon!

Your best friend,

Anne

Respond to the Practice Letter

After you read the practice letter, write your answers to the following questions.

1. To whom is Anne writing the letter? What is her relationship to Anne?

_____

2. From the letter, what do you think is the biggest difference between Anne's old neighborhood and her new neighborhood?

_____

3. What is something that Anne and Kathryn probably used to do together?

_____

4. Whom did Anne meet by the creek?

_____

5. In one or two sentences, summarize Anne's letter. Use these questions to help you write your summary:

   • To whom is the letter written?
   • Why did Anne write the letter?
   • What is the letter about?

_____

_____

_____

_____

Writing Assignment

To write a letter, a writer must think about the purpose of the letter and the person who will receive the letter. Think of a gift that a friend or a loved one has given you. Answer the questions below. Use this writing plan to help you write a first draft on the next page.

What gift were you given?

_____

_____

Who gave you the gift?

_____

_____

Why did he or she give you the gift?

_____

_____

What do you like most about the gift?

_____

_____

First Draft

TIPS FOR WRITING A LETTER:

- Address it to the person you are writing to.
- Indent the first line of the letter.
- State your reason for writing the letter.
- Check for capital letters in the heading, greeting, and closing.

Use your writing plan as a guide to write a thank-you letter. Be sure to tell the person what you like most about the gift.

_____

_____

_____

_____

_____

_____

_____

_____

_____

(Continue on your own paper.)

Revise the Draft

Use the chart below to help you revise your draft. Check YES or NO to answer each question in the chart. If you answer NO, make notes to remind yourself how you can revise, or change, your writing to improve it.

Question	YES ✔	NO ✔	If the answer is NO, what will you do to improve your writing?
Does your letter thank a loved one for a gift he or she has given?			
Does your letter describe what you like about the gift?			
Does your letter have a greeting?			
Does your letter have a closing?			
Do you write the letter from your point of view?			
Have you corrected mistakes in spelling, grammar, and punctuation?			

Use the notes in your chart and your writing plan to revise your draft.

Writing Report Card

Read your revised draft again or ask someone else to read it. Have the person who reads your paper complete the following Report Card. Revise your paper until you have no less than a Very Good Score for each item.

Title of paper: _____

Purpose of paper: _*This is a thank-you letter. It thanks someone for*_

*a gift I received.*

Person who scores the paper: _____

Score	Writing Goals
	Does this letter thank someone for a gift?
	Does the writer describe what he or she likes about the gift?
	Is there a greeting?
	Is there a closing?
	Is the letter written from the writer's point of view?
	Are the letter's grammar, spelling, and punctuation correct?

☺ Excellent Score   ☆ Very Good Score   + Good Score
✔ Acceptable Score   − Needs Improvement

UNIT 4: Paragraph that Describes

HOW MUCH DO YOU KNOW?

Read the paragraph. Then answer the questions.

I just love a parade. I like to see the band march by. The uniforms shine with brass buttons and gold braid. The loud music always makes me want to clap my hands. I also like to see the floats. The floats with storybook characters are the best.

1. What is the topic of the paragraph?

_____

_____

2. Which words describe the band?

_____

_____

3. Write a sentence to add to the paragraph.

_____

_____

_____

Studying a Paragraph that Describes

- A paragraph that describes tells what someone or something is like.
- The topic sentence names the topic.
- The other sentences give details about the topic.

Read the paragraph. Then answer the questions.

Many birds visit my backyard. Red cardinals make nests in our bushes. Many tiny hummingbirds buzz around the flowers in our garden. Robins chirp sweetly to wake me in the morning.

1. What is the topic of the paragraph?

_____

_____

2. Which words tell what the birds are like?

_____

_____

3. Write a sentence to add to the paragraph.

_____

_____

_____

_____

Paying Attention to Details

Good writers use their five senses to study what they will describe. They use words to describe what they notice.

Read each topic. Close your eyes and picture it in your mind. Then write words in the chart to describe the topic.

1. TOPIC: AN ORANGE

looks

_____

_____

feels

_____

_____

tastes

_____

_____

smells

_____

_____

sounds

_____

_____

2. TOPIC: A HAMBURGER

looks

_____

_____

feels

_____

_____

tastes

_____

_____

smells

_____

_____

sounds

_____

_____

Using Colorful Words

Good writers choose colorful words to tell what something is like.

Read the beginning of the paragraph. The topic is kitchens. Write two more detail sentences. Use colorful words. Choose words from the box or use your own words.

cozy
juicy
fresh
delicious
warm
yummy
sweet
shiny

The kitchen is the best room in the house. It smells like homemade bread and spices.

_____

_____

_____

_____

Adding Describing Words to Sentences

Writers can make a sentence clearer. They tell what someone or something is like. Find the nouns. Think of words that describe the nouns to add to each sentence. Write the new sentences.

1. The clown wears a hat.

_____

_____

2. A lion jumps through a hoop.

_____

_____

3. A monkey rides on an elephant.

_____

_____

_____

Proofreading a Paragraph that Describes

PROOFREADING HINTS

- Be sure to indent your paragraph.
- Be sure each sentence begins with a capital letter.
- Check your spelling.

Read the paragraph. Correct at least five mistakes. Use the Proofreading Marks.

PROOFREADING MARKS	
⬭	spell correctly
⊙	add period
?	add question mark
☰	capitalize
ℛ	take out
∧	add
¶	indent paragraph
⌄ ⌄	add quotation marks

Don't you just love a parade? I like to see the band march buy. the uniforms shine with brass buttons and gold braid. The loud musik always makes me want to clap and stamp my feet. i also like to see the floats. The floats with storybook characters are the best. the kings and queens in purple velvet are so beautiful

Write about a Zoo

Draw a picture of a zoo. Make a list of the details in your picture. Then write a sentence that tells the main idea.

_____   _____

_____   _____

_____   _____

MAIN IDEA

_____

_____

_____

Write about a Place You Like

Think of a place you like. Draw a picture of the place. Then write three sentences to describe it.

_____

_____

_____

_____

_____

_____

Describe a Movie

Talk with a friend about a movie you both like. Write the name of the movie. Choose your favorite scene. Write a paragraph that describes your favorite scene.

_____

_____

_____

_____

_____

_____

_____

_____

_____

Describe an Exciting Game

Think of an exciting game that you saw or that you have played. Write four sentences about the game.

_____

_____

_____

_____

_____

_____

_____

_____

A Day at a Lake

Work with a friend. Imagine that you and your friend are having fun at a lake. Think about how it looks, how it smells, and how it sounds. Write four sentences telling what you two do.

_____

_____

_____

_____

_____

_____

_____

_____

Write a Room Riddle

Think about a room in your house or at school. Write sentences to describe it. Do not tell the name of the room. Read your sentences to a friend. Can your friend guess the name of the room?

_____

_____

_____

_____

_____

_____

_____

Write about Bugs

Write four sentences about bugs. Use describing words that tell about the shape and the color of the bugs.

_____

_____

_____

_____

_____

_____

_____

_____

Write about a Snack

Think about a snack you shared with friends. Close your eyes and picture it in your mind. Then write words in the chart to describe the snack.

looks

_____   _____

feels

_____   _____

tastes

_____   _____

smells

_____   _____

Write sentences to describe the snack.

_____

_____

_____

_____

_____

_____

Who Am I?

Draw a picture of yourself sitting at your desk. Then write sentences to go with your picture.

Tell what you can taste, smell, feel, and hear. Use describing words in your sentences.

_____

_____

_____

Write a Travel Report

Write about your city or town. Tell visitors about the special places they can see.

_____

_____

_____

_____

_____

_____

_____

Picture a Place

Think about the places in these pictures. Pick one of the places. Write a paragraph that describes what that place is like.

on a busy street   on a beach

_____

_____

_____

_____

_____

_____

_____

_____

_____

A Practice Descriptive Story

THE RIDE HOME

I leaned forward in my seat and pressed my nose against the cool glass window. I heard the loud final whistle. Grandma and Grandpa waved good-bye to me from the platform. Slowly, the train started to pull away from the station. The car rocked slowly from side to side as it rolled along the tracks.

After a wonderful two-week visit with my grandparents, I was finally going home. I would miss Grandma's snuggly bear hugs and the sweet buttermilk taste of her pancakes. I would miss Grandpa's hearty laugh and the smell of his mint chewing gum as we talked while doing jigsaw puzzles together.

With a big smile, I sat back in the cozy seat and looked out the window. I watched as we passed through the rolling hills and fresh country air. The train headed back toward the city. My eyelids began to get heavy and I drifted off to sleep. When I woke up, Mom and Dad were there to welcome me home.

Respond to the Practice Descriptive Story

After you read "The Ride Home," write your answers to the following questions.

1. What type of transportation was the writer taking?

_____

2. Whom had the writer recently visited?

_____

3. What senses did the writer use to describe things in the story?

_____

4. What are two descriptions that the writer used to help you experience what was happening in the story?

_____

_____

5. In one or two sentences, summarize the story. Use these questions to help you write your summary:

   • What is the story about?
   • What happens first? Second?
   • How does the story end?

_____

_____

_____

Writing Assignment

To describe something, a writer tells what he or she sees, hears, feels, tastes, and smells. The writer uses interesting words. Think about the best birthday party you ever had. Then use this writing plan to help you write a first draft on the next page.

Around the circle, write words that describe what you <u>saw</u>, <u>heard</u>, <u>felt</u>, <u>smelled</u>, and <u>tasted</u> at your birthday party.

Urban Air

Trampoline Park

dodge ball

MY BEST BIRTHDAY PARTY

big slide

music

Happy

cake

pizza

First Draft

TIPS FOR WRITING A DESCRIPTIVE STORY:

- Help readers see, smell, taste, feel, and hear what you are writing about.
- Use interesting words to help you describe.

Use your writing plan as a guide for writing a descriptive story. Include a catchy title.

at MY berthday I saw a bigsiide it wascool and I herd music I like the music and Ife lt relex Happey and I smeld cake and I tasted pizza.

(Continue on your own paper.)

Revise the Draft

Use the chart below to help you revise your draft. Check YES or NO to answer each question in the chart. If you answer NO, make notes to remind yourself how you can revise, or change, your writing to improve it.

Question	YES ✔	NO ✔	If the answer is NO, what will you do to improve your writing?
Does your story tell about a birthday party you have had?			
Does your story describe what happens in order?			
Do you use action words to describe what happens?			
Does your story describe what you see, hear, smell, taste, and feel?			
Have you corrected mistakes in spelling, grammar, and punctuation?			

Use the notes in your chart and your writing plan to revise your draft.

Writing Report Card

Read your revised draft again or ask someone else to read it. Have the person who reads your paper complete the following Report Card. Revise your paper until you have no less than a Very Good Score for each item.

Title of paper: _____

Purpose of paper: _*This is a descriptive story. It describes a*_

*birthday party I had.*

Person who scores the paper: _____

Score	Writing Goals
	Does this story tell about a birthday party the writer had?
	Does it describe what happens in order?
	Are there action words to describe what happens?
	Does it describe what the writer saw, heard, smelled, tasted, and felt?
	Is the story written from the writer's point of view?
	Are the story's grammar, spelling, and punctuation correct?

☺ Excellent Score   ☆ Very Good Score   + Good Score

✔ Acceptable Score   – Needs Improvement

UNIT 5: Story

HOW MUCH DO YOU KNOW?

Read the story. Then answer the questions.

A LONG NIGHT

    Lateisha got into bed. She lay down, but she was too tired to sleep. She tried counting sheep. She tried reading a book. Nothing worked.

    At six o'clock in the morning, Lateisha gave up and got out of bed. She showered and dressed. When she started to eat her cereal, Mother asked why Lateisha was up so early. Mother told her it was Saturday. Without saying a word, Lateisha went back to bed.

1. What is the title?

_____

2. What is the problem?

_____

_____

3. Who are the characters?

_____

_____

Studying a Story

> - A story has a beginning, a middle, and an ending.
> - A story is often about solving a problem.
> - A story has a title.

Read the story. Then answer the questions.

THE HOLE

One day a small boy was walking down the street. Suddenly, he fell down a hole. It was a very deep, dark hole. The small boy couldn't see. He was really scared. What did he do? He fell asleep, of course!

A few hours later, the boy was awakened by singing. The voices were high-pitched and squeaky. Then the boy saw hundreds of tiny candles.

They were being carried by hundreds of tiny mice. They led him to an underground elevator. The boy went up. He was back on the street!

1. What is the title? _____

2. Who are the characters? _____

3. What is the problem? _____

4. How is the problem solved? _____

_____

Thinking about What Might Happen

- Good writers create an interesting problem in the beginning of a story.

- Then they plan what will happen to solve the problem.

Read the beginning of the story.
Then fill in the chart.

A BIRTHDAY SURPRISE

　　Aunt Sally will be ninety years old tomorrow. She has lived a long time, and she is very wise. My older sister and I want to do something special for Aunt Sally's birthday. We plan to bake her the most beautiful birthday cake she has ever seen. Every time we go into the kitchen, though, Aunt Sally is there!

PROBLEM

_____

_____

HOW TO SOLVE

_____

_____

Using Enough Details

> Good writers use enough details to help readers picture what happens in a story.

Read the paragraph. Then write it again. Add details to tell what John sees.

John could feel the plane taking off. He looked out the window.

_____

_____

_____

_____

_____

_____

_____

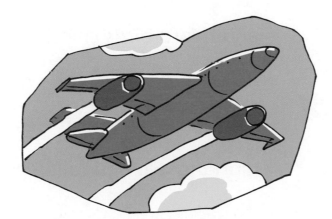

Proofreading a Story

PROOFREADING HINTS

- Be sure each sentence begins with a capital letter.
- Be sure each sentence ends with an end mark.
- Check your spelling.

PROOFREADING MARKS

⬭	spell correctly
⊙	add period
?	add question mark
≡	capitalize
℘	take out
∧	add
¶	indent paragraph
ⱽ ⱽ	add quotation marks

Read the story. Correct at least six mistakes. Use the Proofreading Marks.

WHAT A DAY!

Arnold climbed the stairs. he was very tired. School had been tuff that day. The soccer game had been tuffer.

Arnold got into bed. He lay down, but he could not fall asleep. he was thinking about he soccer game and the goal he missed

Arnold felt himself kicking the ball into the goal. Suddenly, he felt cold and heard birds chirping. he looked down and saw that he had kicked off the blanket. The sun was up and it was morning. He had fallen asleep after all!

A Story about Foxes

Read the sentences. Then tell what the foxes do next. Finish the story.

Two foxes walk to the park. They sit on a bench. They eat their lunch.

_____

_____

_____

_____

_____

_____

Write about Being a Rabbit

Read the story. Then write a story about what else could happen to Pinky, Spot, and Fluffy.

My favorite movie is on now. Real rabbits are in the movie. Their names are Pinky, Spot, and Fluffy. Once, Spot got his tail stuck in a fence. Pinky and Fluffy helped him.

_____

_____

_____

_____

_____

_____

_____

Write about Waiting

Think of a time you had to wait for someone else. Write a story about what happened.

_____

_____

_____

_____

_____

_____

_____

_____

_____

_____

Finish the Story

Read the story. What do you think is in the bag? What do you think happens next? Finish the story. Tell what happens.

    Last night I saw a huge monster. I saw a bag in the monster's hand. The monster gave me the bag. I saw something funny inside. I gave it to my sister.

_____

_____

_____

_____

_____

_____

_____

Write a Story Beginning

Write good beginning sentences for a story about going into outer space. Draw a picture to go with your sentences.

_____

_____

_____

_____

_____

Write Animal Facts

Draw a picture of an animal. Then use the sentences below to write about it. Write exact words in place of the underlined words.

The <u>animal</u> can <u>move</u>. The <u>animal</u> eats <u>food</u>.

_____

_____

_____

_____

Characters and Settings

Look at the pictures below. Look at the settings. Choose one character and one setting. Use them to write a story.

CHARACTERS

Sammy Seal

Shawn

Kim

SETTINGS

on a planet in the future
yesterday on a farm
at a beach in winter

_____

_____

_____

_____

_____

_____

Solving a Problem

Many stories have an interesting problem that must be solved. Read the story. With a friend, write an ending to the story.

You make friends with a dinosaur and bring it to school. The dinosaur does not know how to act in school.

_____

_____

_____

_____

_____

_____

_____

A Practice Problem-and-Solution Story

JUMP IN!

Juan knew he was going to have a great summer when he and his best friend, Danny, arrived at camp. Everywhere he looked, there were tons of boys his age, laughing together, playing tennis, or swimming at the pool. Juan and Danny quickly found their cabin and met their camp counselor. After they unpacked their suitcases, the boys decided to go for a swim. They changed into their swimsuits and walked down to the pool.

At first, Juan and Danny stayed in the shallow end. They played games and splashed in the water with a few other boys. Every now and then, Juan watched other boys jump, dive, and do flips off the diving board, but he did not feel brave enough to try it himself.

After a while, Danny said that they should take turns jumping off the diving board. Juan looked nervously at

Danny and shook his head. Danny smiled and told Juan that it was not as scary as it looked. Juan finally agreed to give it a try. Slowly, he climbed to the top of the diving board. He took a few steps to the end of the board and looked over at Danny. Danny gave him a big smile. Juan took a deep breath, closed his eyes, and jumped. He hit the water with a splash and bobbed up to the surface. He was grinning from ear to ear. Juan and Danny spent the rest of the day jumping off the diving board!

Respond to the Practice Problem-and-Solution Story

After you read "Jump In!," write your answers to the following questions.

1. Where did Juan and Danny go?

_____

2. What did they do just before they walked to the pool?

_____

3. What was the problem in the story?

_____

4. How was the problem solved?

_____

5. How did Juan feel at the end of the story?

_____

6. In one or two sentences, summarize the story. Use these questions to help you write your summary:

   • What is the story about?
   • What happens first? Second?
   • How does the story end?

_____

_____

_____

Writing Assignment

A story often reveals a problem that a character has, and then the solution. Think up a character who has a problem. Answer the questions below. Use this writing plan to help you write a first draft on the next page.

Who is the character in your story?

What is your character's problem?

How is the problem solved?

What are the events that happen in your story? (first, next, last)

How does the character feel at the end of the story?

First Draft

TIPS FOR WRITING A PROBLEM-AND-SOLUTION STORY:

- Think about the problem that your story reveals.
- Check to see that the story shows the solution to the problem.

Use your writing plan as a guide for writing a problem-and-solution story. Include a catchy title.

_____

_____

_____

_____

_____

_____

_____

(Continue on your own paper.)

Revise the Draft

Use the chart below to help you revise your draft. Check YES or NO to answer each question in the chart. If you answer NO, make notes to remind yourself how you can revise, or change, your writing to improve it.

Question	YES ✔	NO ✔	If the answer is NO, what will you do to improve your writing?
Does your story identify a problem?			
Does your story have a solution?			
Does your story have a beginning, middle, and end?			
Does your story tell the events in order?			
Have you corrected mistakes in spelling, grammar, and punctuation?			

Use the notes in your chart and your writing plan to revise your draft.

Writing Report Card

Read your revised draft again or ask someone else to read it. Have the person who reads your paper complete the following Report Card. Revise your paper until you have no less than a Very Good Score for each item.

Title of paper: _____

Purpose of paper: *This is a problem and solution story. It shows how a* _____

character solves a problem. _____

Person who scores the paper: _____

Score	Writing Goals
	Does this story identify a problem?
	Does it have a solution?
	Are there action words to describe what happens?
	Is there a beginning, middle, and end?
	Are events told in order?
	Are the story's grammar, spelling, and punctuation correct?

☺ Excellent Score ☆ Very Good Score + Good Score

 Acceptable Score – Needs Improvement

UNIT 6: How-to Paragraph

HOW MUCH DO YOU KNOW?

Read the paragraph. Then answer the questions.

Sewing on a button can be easy. First, get a needle and thread. You will also need the button and a piece of clothing. Choose a thread color to match the clothing. Next, thread the needle. Then, sew on the button tightly. Last, make a knot in the thread. Cut the thread.

1. What is the topic sentence?

_____

_____

2. What is the first step?

_____

_____

3. What things do you need to sew on a button?

_____

_____

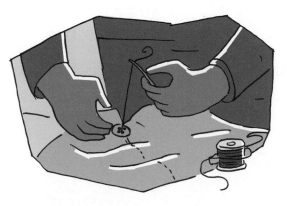

Studying a How-to Paragraph

- A how-to paragraph tells how to make or do something.
- The topic sentence names the topic of the paragraph.
- The detail sentences explain the steps in order.
- The paragraph is indented.

Read the paragraph. Draw a line under the topic sentence. Then draw a circle around the words that tell the order of the steps.

    This is a simple way to wrap a gift. First, get wrapping paper, scissors, and tape. Next, cut the paper to fit all the way around the gift. Then, put the paper together around the middle of the gift. Tape the paper. Last, fold the paper up and over the ends of the gift. Tape it closed.

Write the things you need to wrap a gift.

_____

_____

_____

Connecting Ideas in Sequence

In a how-to paragraph, good writers tell the steps in the correct order.

Look at the pictures. Then write the four steps.

HOW TO MAKE SOUP

1.

_____

_____

2.

_____

_____

3.

_____

_____

4.

_____

_____

Getting the Reader's Interest

> Good writers use good beginning sentences
> to interest their readers.

Read the story beginnings. Draw a line under the better one.

1. a. Albert waded through the swamp. The alligator was close behind him. Albert's heart pounded like a drum.

   b. Albert walked in the swamp. An alligator was following him. Albert felt scared.

2. a. The skyscraper was tall and shiny. It looked like a steel box against the sky. I thought it was beautiful.

   b. The building was tall and gray. It stood out against the sky. It was interesting to look at.

3. a. One day we walked into a garden.

   b. One day we tiptoed into a strange garden. There were giant red and yellow flowers everywhere.

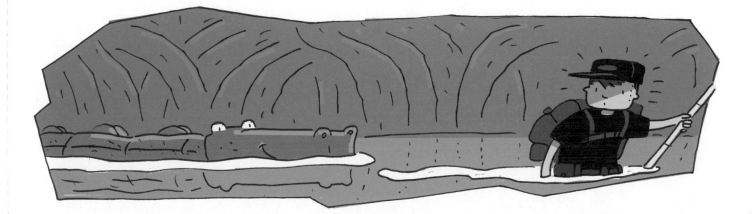

Joining Sentences

> Writers often join two sentences into one.
> The new sentence says the same thing in fewer words.

Read each pair of sentences. Use the word **and** to join the two sentences into one. You may need to change the verb to go with your new sentence. The first one is done for you.

1. Bob likes to sled. Jasmine likes to sled.

Bob and Jasmine like to sled.

2. Tran goes with them. Carlos goes with them.

3. Carlos packs a lunch. Bob packs a lunch.

4. Bob sleds all day. Jasmine sleds all day.

5. Bob is tired. Jasmine is tired.

Proofreading a How-to Paragraph

PROOFREADING HINTS

- Be sure you indent your paragraph.
- Be sure each sentence begins with a capital letter.
- Be sure each sentence ends with an end mark.

Read the how-to paragraph. Use the Proofreading Marks to correct at least eight mistakes.

PROOFREADING MARKS	
⬭	spell correctly
⊙	add period
?	add question mark
≡	capitalize
℘	take out
∧	add
¶	indent paragraph
ⱱ ⱱ	add quotation marks

sewing on a button can be eazy. First, get a needle and thread. you will also need the button and peece of clothing Choose a thread color to match the clothing. next, thread the needle then, sew on the button tightly. Last, make a knot in the thread. Cut the thread

Write the topic sentence correctly.

_____

_____

How to Play a Game

Work with a friend or two. Imagine that you are at a playground. You are going to play a playground game. Write a paragraph telling how to play the game.

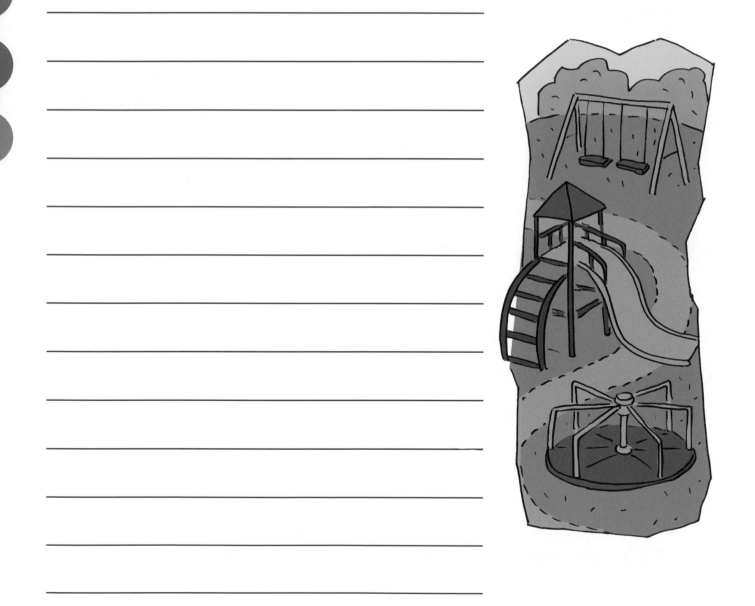

_____

_____

_____

_____

_____

_____

_____

_____

_____

_____

Write about a Job

Think of a job you have to do. Draw a picture of yourself doing that job. Write sentences telling how to do the job.

_____

_____

_____

_____

_____

_____

Plan a Garden

Work with a friend. Draw a picture of a garden you would both like. Write sentences that tell how you would make the garden.

_____

_____

_____

_____

_____

_____

Write about Work

Think of someone who has a job. Write sentences about what that person does at work. Tell how that person does one part of the job.

_____

_____

_____

_____

_____

_____

_____

_____

_____

_____

Write about School

Think of something you and your friends do at school.
Write directions for another student to follow.

_____

_____

_____

_____

_____

_____

_____

_____

Write about Clown School

Imagine that you go to a school to learn to be a clown. Write sentences to tell a friend how to be a clown.

_____

_____

_____

_____

_____

_____

_____

Make a How-to Poster

Think about how you would do a chore, such as making a bed or washing the dishes. Picture the chore in four steps. Draw how to do a step in each part of this poster. Write a sentence for each step.

1.

_____

_____

2.

_____

_____

3.

_____

_____

4.

_____

_____

How to Make a Chocolate Milkshake

The pictures below show the steps to make a chocolate milkshake. In order, write what is happening in each picture. Use sequence words such as <u>first</u>, <u>next</u>, <u>then</u>, and <u>last</u> to help you.

_____

_____

_____

_____

_____

_____

_____

A Practice How-to Paragraph

Wendy is making a cake. She follows the directions on the back of the cake mix box. Here are the directions.

MAKING A CAKE

First, preheat oven to 350 degrees. Then pour the cake mix into a large bowl. Add two eggs to the bowl. Next, stir in water and vegetable oil. Mix the batter for two minutes with an electric mixer on low speed. Pour the batter into a lightly floured pan. Last, bake the cake in the oven for 30 minutes. Take the cake out of the oven and allow it to cool completely before icing.

Respond to the How-to Paragraph

After reading "Making a Cake," write your answers to the following questions.

1. At what temperature should the oven be set?

_____

2. What should you do after adding water and vegetable oil?

_____

3. For how long should the cake bake in the oven?

_____

4. What should you do before icing the cake?

_____

Writing Assignment

Think about the things you need and the steps you follow when you brush your teeth. Use this writing plan to help you write a first draft on the next page.

1. What will you need to brush your teeth?

_____

2. Write four steps you follow when you brush your teeth.

Step 1

Step 2

Step 3

Step 4

First Draft

TIPS FOR WRITING A HOW-TO PARAGRAPH:

- Choose one thing to teach someone.
- Think of all the materials you will need.
- Think of all the steps someone will follow.
- Use sequence words.

Use your writing plan as a guide for writing your first draft of a how-to paragraph. Include a catchy title.

_____

_____

_____

_____

_____

_____

_____

_____

(Continue on your own paper.)

Revise the Draft

Use the chart below to help you revise your draft. Check YES or NO to answer each question in the chart. If you answer NO, make notes to remind yourself how you can revise, or change, your writing to improve it.

Question	YES ✔	NO ✔	If the answer is NO, what will you do to improve your writing?
Does your paragraph teach the reader how to brush his or her teeth?			
Does your paragraph include the materials the person needs?			
Does your paragraph tell the steps someone must follow?			
Are the steps in order?			
Do you use sequence words, such as <u>first</u>, <u>next</u>, <u>then</u>, and <u>last</u>?			
Have you corrected mistakes in spelling, grammar, and punctuation?			

Use the notes in your chart and your writing plan to revise your draft.

Writing Report Card

Read your revised draft again or ask someone else to read it. Have the person who reads your paper complete the following Report Card. Revise your paper until you have no less than a Very Good Score for each item.

Title of paper: _____

Purpose of paper: _*This is a how-to paragraph. It tells someone how to*_

*brush his or her teeth.*

Person who scores the paper: _____

Score	Writing Goals
	Does this paragraph teach you how to brush your teeth?
	Does it tell you what materials you need?
	Does it tell you the steps you must follow?
	Are the steps in order?
	Are there sequence words, such as <u>first</u>, <u>next</u>, <u>then</u>, and <u>last</u>?
	Are the paragraph's grammar, spelling, and punctuation correct?

☺ Excellent Score   ☆ Very Good Score   + Good Score

✔ Acceptable Score   − Needs Improvement

Answer Key

Answers to the practice paper exercises questions may vary, but examples are provided here to give you an idea of how your child may respond.

Unit 1: Sentence about a Picture

p. 6
1. The girl eats pizza.
2. The robot walks a dog.
3. cereal

p. 7
1. The balloon goes up.
2. The room is a mess!
3. It's a windy fall day.
4. The girls are ready to eat.

p. 8
1. fruit bowl, 2 eggs, 1 glass
   One person will eat breakfast.
2. ticket booth, roller coaster, Ferris wheel, children.
The fair is open!

p. 9
1. Chimpanzees
2. hunting
3. Bananas
4. yellow
5. leap

p. 10
1. <u>bears</u> are big animals.
2. They may weigh 1,000 pounds○
3. <u>some</u> live in cold places○
4. <u>others</u> like warm weather.

Unit 2: Personal Story

p. 24
Circle: first, then, last of all
My family had fun at the summer fair yesterday.

p. 25
Underline: I, we, my, our
Circle: first, then, after, last of all

p. 26
Underline: In one movie I saw deer, bears, and foxes in a forest. Another movie was a cartoon about mice and pigs. The best animal movie I ever saw took place in the jungle. It was about a parrot that saved a tiger's life.
Topic sentence: I like many movies about animals.
Sentence added: Sentences will vary. Be sure that the detail supports the topic.

p. 27
1. dash
2. boxes
3. apples
4. fuzzy
5. cheerful
6. giggle

p. 28
   One day my family and I went to an apple orchard. <u>we</u> went to pick fresh apples. <u>first, i</u> got a big basket. <u>next,</u> I picked some ripe apples off the trees ○ I put them in the basket ○ After about an hour, <u>i</u> was too hungry to keep going.

that's when <u>i</u> bit into a juicy, red apple○ The sweet, ripe apple tasted better than anything else in the world.

p. 38
1. He competed in the school spelling bee.
2. He said his palms got sweaty.
3. akrobat
4. No. The last sentence says he did not win.
5. The writer felt a little disappointed.
6. Be sure your child correctly summarizes the significant events in the story, paraphrasing as needed. Summaries should be organized in a thoughtful way, with the main ideas and important details clearly presented in order. Spelling, punctuation, capitalization, and grammar should be correct.

Unit 3: Friendly Letter
p. 43
1. green: October 22, 2005
2. blue: Juan
3. red: Love,
4. Juan

p. 44
1. red: July 27, 2005
2. yellow: Your friend,

3. blue: Dear Chris,

4. orange: Richard

5. green: body of letter

p. 45

Responses will vary. Be sure that pictures are complete and that sentences tell about the pictures.

p. 46

1. her grandmother

2. to thank her

3. Possible responses: The pink roses are her favorite flowers. Emily feels much better now.

p. 47

2. He dances and sings.

3. Andy writes plays and acts them out.

4. He gets applause and cheers.

p. 48

February 7, 2005

dear Tanya ∧

I had fun at your house last week! I'm so (bezy) _busy_ at school now. I'm in the class play. I'm a bear in the play⊙ My costume is brown and fuzzy. have you ever been in a play?

your friend ∧

Brenda

p. 57

1. Kathryn, best friend

2. Her new neighborhood is in the country.

3. They probably used to ride bikes together.

4. Shannon

5. Be sure your child correctly summarizes the significant events in the story, paraphrasing as needed. Summaries should be organized in a thoughtful way, with the main ideas and important details clearly presented in order. Spelling, punctuation, capitalization, and grammar should be correct.

Unit 4: Paragraph that Describes

p. 62

1. I just love a parade.

2. uniforms shine with brass buttons and gold braid, loud music always makes me want to clap my hands

3. Sentences will vary. Be sure that the detail supports the topic.

p. 63

Possible responses:

1. Many birds visit my backyard.

2. red, tiny, buzz, sweetly

3. Sentences will vary. Be sure that the sentence supports the topic.

p. 64

Responses will vary. Be sure each response is a detail that supports the topic and is categorized correctly.

p. 65

Responses will vary. Be sure the detail sentences include vivid adjectives.

p. 66

Responses will vary. Be sure each sentence includes adjectives.

p. 67

¶ Don't you just love a parade? I like to see the band march (buy.) _by_

the uniforms shine with brass buttons and gold braid. The loud (musik) _music_ always makes me want to clap and stamp my feet. i also like to see the floats. The floats with storybook characters are the best. the kings and queens in purple velvet are so beautiful⊙

p. 81

1. The writer was on a train.

2. The writer had visited his or her grandparents.

3. sight, sound, smell, taste, and touch

4. Answer may include any two of the following: cool glass window; loud final whistle, car rocked slowly from side to side; snuggly bear hugs; sweet buttermilk taste; hearty laugh, mint chewing gum; cozy seat; green hills and fresh country air

5. Be sure your child correctly summarizes the significant events in the story, paraphrasing as needed. Summaries should be organized in a thoughtful way, with the main ideas and important details clearly presented in order. Spelling, punctuation, capitalization, and grammar should be correct.

Unit 5: Story

p. 86

1. A Long Night

2. Lateisha couldn't sleep.

3. Lateisha, Mother

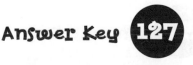
Answer Key 127

p. 87

1. The Hole
2. a boy, tiny mice
3. The boy falls down a hole.
4. The mice show the boy a way out.

p. 88

Problem: Aunt Sally is in the kitchen.

How to Solve: Responses will vary. Accept all responses that tell a way to solve the problem.

p. 89

Responses will vary. Be sure responses include enough details to tell clearly what John sees.

p. 90

Arnold climbed the stairs. he was very tired. School had been *tough* (tuff) that day. The soccer game had been (tuffer.) *tougher*

Arnold got into bed. He lay down, but he could not fall asleep. he was thinking about (he) *the* soccer game and the goal he missed⊙

Arnold felt himself kicking the ball into the goal. Suddenly, he felt cold and heard birds chirping. he looked down and saw that he had kicked off the blanket. The sun was up and it was morning. He had fallen asleep after all!

p. 101

1. They went to summer camp.
2. They changed into their swimsuits.
3. Juan was afraid to go off the diving board.
4. Danny convinced him to try it.
5. He was happy.
6. Be sure your child correctly summarizes the significant events in the story, paraphrasing as needed. Summaries should be organized in a thoughtful way, with the main ideas and important details clearly presented in order. Spelling, punctuation, capitalization, and grammar should be correct.

Unit 6: How-to Paragraph

p. 106

1. Sewing on a button can be easy.
2. First, get a needle and thread.
3. needle, thread, button, piece of clothing

p. 107

Underline: This is a simple way to wrap a gift.
Circle: First, Next, Then, Last
Things you need: wrapping paper, scissors, tape

p. 108

Possible responses:
1. First, get a can of soup, a can opener, and a pot.
2. Next, open the soup can.
3. Then, pour the soup into the pot.
4. Last, heat the soup.

p. 109

1. a
2. a
3. b

p. 110

2. Tran and Carlos go with them.

3. Carlos and Bob pack a lunch.
4. Bob and Jasmine sled all day.
5. Bob and Jasmine are tired.

p. 111

¶ sewing on a button can be (eazy.) *easy*

First, get a needle and thread. you will also need the button and (peece) of clothing⊙ Choose a *piece* thread color to match the clothing. next, thread the needle⊙ then, sew on the button tightly. Last, make a knot in the thread. Cut the thread⊙

p. 121

1. 350 degrees
2. mix the batter with an electric mixer
3. 30 minutes
4. allow the cake to cool